Why Me?

Comfort for
the Victimized

Resources for Changing Lives

A Ministry of
THE CHRISTIAN COUNSELING AND
EDUCATIONAL FOUNDATION
Glenside, Pennsylvania

RCL Ministry Booklets
Susan Lutz, Series Editor

Why Me?

Comfort for
the Victimized

David Powlison

P&R
PUBLISHING
P.O. BOX 817 • PHILLIPSBURG • NEW JERSEY 08865-0817

Scripture quotations are from the *NEW AMERICAN STANDARD BIBLE®*. ©Copyright The Lockman Foundation 1960, 1962, 1963, 1968, 1971, 1972 1973, 1975, 1977, 1995. Used by permission.

Printed in the United States of America

Library of Congress Cataloging-in-Publication Data

Powlison, David, 1949-
        Why me? : comfort for the victimized / David Powlison.
                p.   cm. — (Resources for changing lives)
        Includes bibliographical references.
        ISBN 0-87552-695-0 (pbk.)
        1. Bible. O.T. Psalms X—Meditations.
        2. Victims—Prayer-books and devotions—
        English. 3. Consolation. I. Title. II. Series.

        BS145010th .P69 2003
        248.8'6—dc21
                                                2003042457

Why do You stand afar off, O LORD?
Why do You hide in times of trouble?
In pride the wicked burn, pursuing the af-
　　　flicted.
They are caught in the plots which they
　　　have devised.
For the wicked boasts of his heart's
　　　desire.
The greedy man curses and spurns the
　　　LORD.
The wicked, in the haughtiness of his
　　　countenance, does not seek Him.
All his thoughts are, "There is no God."
His ways prosper at all times.
Your judgments are on high, out of his
　　　sight.
As for all his adversaries, he snorts at
　　　them.
He says to himself, "I will not be moved;
throughout all generations I will not be in
　　　adversity."
His mouth is full of curses and deceit and
　　　oppression;
under his tongue is trouble and wickedness.

He sits in the lurking places of the villages.
In the hiding places he kills the innocent.
His eyes stealthily watch for the unfortunate.
He lurks in a hiding place as a lion in his
      lair.
He lurks to catch the afflicted.
He catches the afflicted when he draws
      him into his net.
He crouches, he bows down,
and the unfortunate fall by his mighty
      ones.
He says to himself, "God has forgotten.
He has hidden His face. He will never see
      it."
Arise, O LORD. O God, lift up Your hand.
Do not forget the afflicted.
Why has the wicked spurned God?
He has said to himself, "You will not re-
      quire it."
You have seen it, for You have beheld
      trouble and vexation to take it
      into Your hand.
The unfortunate commits himself to You.
You have been the helper of the orphan.
Break the arm of the wicked and the evil-
      doer.
Seek out his wickedness until You find none.
The LORD is King forever and ever.

Nations have perished from His land.
O Lord, You have heard the desire of the
afflicted.
You will strengthen their heart.
You will incline Your ear to vindicate the
orphan and the oppressed,
so that man who is of the earth will no
longer cause terror.

Psalm 10

Helen had been betrayed by her husband. He had played the part of the dutiful, church-going husband, father, and provider for many years. But unbeknownst to Helen, he had maintained mistresses in three cities. Helen had trusted him with all the family finances, including a half million dollars she had inherited. He siphoned off all her money into his name. He spent much of it and ran up debts besides, financing a lifestyle of gambling and immorality. Helen had been ignorant of this, but she was not unaware of other evils. For many years, she had been forced to commit sexual acts she found repellent. In public her husband's demeanor was good-natured, but in private he would berate her and threaten to beat her. He routinely called her names and blamed her for every problem.

Helen suffered in silence until bankruptcy broke his secret life into the open. Helen was a believer who had sought God as her refuge amid the sexual and verbal abuse. But when everything exploded, she felt unprotected and insecure. All along, genuine faith in God had intertwined with her tendencies toward keeping up appearances: "Put up with it, pretend it's not really happening, and everything's okay." Now she couldn't pretend. She was in trouble.

What should she say? How should she think? What should she do? Where is God amid such devastation? God knows our hearts; he anticipates these questions in a time of storm. And his Word speaks hope, power, and comfort to those in such situations. Psalm 10, for example, was written for those who have been victimized by others. It was written for Helen. It is a message of anguish and refuge. It is *not* about pretending, but about facing reality and truth.

Helen must pick up many pieces. She needs the daily comfort of pastor and friends. She needs the church to play grace-giving hardball with her husband about his sins. (He skipped town two weeks later and moved in with one of the mistresses, and was excommunicated for his impenitence.) Helen needs legal advice, immediate financial help, and financial counsel about what to do next. She needs to find out if she has a sexually transmitted disease. She needs to praise God, to hear the Word of life, to participate in the Lord's Supper, to pray with others. She needs counsel to console her and to nourish good fruits already present: faith, buds of forgiveness, and love. She needs counsel to deal with bitterness, fear, and unbelief. Most of all, Helen needs to know that God is present, powerful, listening, just, caring, and understanding. She needs God to do something.

Psalm 10 is for Helen. It is also for the family in Sri Lanka that wonders where the next terrorist bombing might occur. It is for the young man who was molested in boarding school. It is for the pastor facing church members who are out to get him. It is for the factory worker being persecuted for her faith, and the college student whose professor has an ax to grind against God. It is for the family that lives in a high crime neighborhood, and the widow cheated by a home-repair scam. It is for anyone under assault in a world where many people wish to use us and harm us.

Psalm 10 guides a person into knowing

God in the midst of being violated. How can Helen—and you—make these words and experiences your own? Think of a psalm as a "four-part harmony" and savor the layers of significance and reservoirs of power that fill the Word of God. Join the four-part chorus; don't think that you sing or pray alone.

The Psalm's Four Voices

The first voice in the psalm calls out the experience of the writer. Psalm 10 was written about three thousand years ago by a sufferer who called on the Lord. Yes, the truths are universal, part of God's Word for all ages and people. But first they were *personal*, written by a man who felt abandoned, overwhelmed, and outraged in the face of evils. Yet he knew God, so he worked through his experience in relationship to him. This psalm's ideas about evil, hurt, and God's love and power arise in heartfelt conversation with that good and powerful Person. Helen can listen in on someone else's heart, someone else's conversation with God.

A second voice sounds the experience of God's people through all ages. Israel and the church have *suffered together* in this fallen world. Your individual experience is part of a larger whole, God's new society. The Lord—Yahweh, Jesus—is the hope of all the afflicted and needy, all the poor in spirit. Countless others have made this psalm their own. You are part of a choir, and sometimes others can carry the tune while you catch your breath.

The third voice registers Jesus' experience. He expressed these sentiments as a man of sorrows, acquainted with grief. Your individual experience is the subset of his experience, if you are *in Christ*. Imagine! You can love the Jesus who felt, thought, and said these things. Psalm 10 expresses the inner life and words of a Person that Helen—and you—can grow to love.

Finally, *you*, the reader, weigh in with the fourth voice. These words are meant to map onto *your* experience. Helen found that her experience could be expressed in ways she'd never think of herself. The Word of God comes to change us and our response to our own lives.

Psalm 10 contains two things: honest requests and thoughtful analysis. At the beginning and end, the injured person bluntly talks to God: "Why are you far away? Get up and do something. You see what's going on. Sufferers trust you because you've helped the helpless in the past. Strip the power away from the hurtful now. I know you hear what I want. I know you will listen and make things right." In the middle, the sufferer vividly describes people who harm others—how they think and act and affect innocent victims. People who harm *people* are also rebelling against *God*. They will be destroyed.

Psalm 10 unfolds in four movements: a cry of desolation, a blunt assessment of predatory people, a cry of reliance on God, and a confident affirmation. Here are the details.[1]

I. Opening Cry: Where Are You? (v. 1)

Why do You stand afar off, O LORD? Why do You hide in times of trouble?

Where *are* you? Where *were* you? Often this is the heart's first cry: "You have said that you love me, so why do you seem absent just when I am violated? Why don't I know your protection?"

This is a cry of faith. Jesus said almost identical words as his faith expressed its anguish: "My God, my God, why have You forsaken me?" (Ps. 22:1; Matt. 27:46). You are in the company of one who knows God yet has felt abandoned.

People can ask questions like these from

two fundamentally different stances. For those who walk in the footsteps of this psalm, the questions express a cry of faith that looks to God. In trouble, they *want* God but feel overwhelmed and isolated. Other people express a cry of unbelief, hatred, and accusation. In trouble, they *blame* God. At first, it may not be clear which stance predominates. There may be mixed motives. Helen groped in God's direction, wondering at times if God wasn't a figment of her imagination. "I believe, help my unbelief." But over time it always becomes clear whether we are processing our anguish through faith or through pride and unbelief. Psalm 10:1 speaks intimately and directly with trust in the Lord who is great, not with contempt for a god who seems impotent and uncaring.

II. Analyze Harmful People: They Are Proud, Willful, Godless, and Predatory (vv. 2–11)

In pride the wicked burn, pursuing the afflicted.
No psalm gives a fuller description of the inner workings of those who hurt others. The afflicted man spells out why he is distressed. Why? It helps to describe what you are up

against. Hurtful people are self-ruled and self-exalting: "proud." They are consumed with and by the things they do to others: they "burn."[2] This burning describes the arousal of any evil desire. Even at the mildest level a dark passion operates: "You stupid !@#$% jerk! You are useless! I wish you'd never been born" (sanitized quotation of a father's response to a son's mistake while working in the family store). More extreme violence rages with the same fire. The burning can be sexual or financial: the lust of the powerful or the single-minded pursuit of a scam. Evildoers exalt themselves and their own agenda. In each case, someone with power picks on the helpless to further his own self-interest.

They [the afflicted] are caught in the plots which they [the wicked] have devised.[3]

The word "plots" vividly describes the fact that people *think about* using and abusing others. Violence and betrayal are not accidental. Helen's husband set out to destroy her marital and financial well-being.

For the wicked boasts of his heart's desire. The greedy man curses and spurns the LORD.

Simply put, evildoers do what they want.

They are not "sick," except in a metaphorical sense. They are *wicked* and live for their cravings.

Notice that to serve self-centered desire excludes serving the Lord. Abusers of others are rebels against God. They turn *from* the Lord *to* their greed. The sufferer's plight reveals that those who caused the suffering have a problem with God. Something bigger is going on behind someone's particular miseries.

The wicked, in the haughtiness of his countenance, does not seek Him. All his thoughts are, "There is no God."

Imagine living inside a mind in which there are no thoughts about God—except for the thought that "God doesn't matter"! The plans, memories, assessments, hopes, attitudes, reactions . . . are devoid of God's will, God's judgment, his mercy and lordship. A person who seeks only what he instinctively craves is by definition "wicked." Helen's husband pursued his own agenda, indifferent to what it looked like to God. The psalmist reminds himself and God what such people are really like. It helps to know that those who oppress *me* have really got a problem with God. It helps in bringing the problem to God as a matter of his concern.

His ways prosper at all times. Your judgments are on high, out of his sight. As for all his adversaries, he snorts at them. He says to himself, "I will not be moved; throughout all generations I will not be in adversity."

Users seem to "get away with it"—in the short run. Their ways apparently "prosper." While Helen picks up the pieces, her husband runs off with a job, money, girlfriend, freedom, and self-righteous superiority to small-minded church busybodies: "I will not be moved." Violators think, "My life works, and nobody can stop me." Helen's husband can skip town and never look back—he thinks.

This presumption is wired into the wicked act itself. Neither fear nor love hinders the wicked's self-centeredness. Understanding these thought processes can help Helen. It can keep her relying on God rather than blaming him. It keeps her moral compass rightly aligned. Notice that even in analyzing evil, the sufferer talks *to* God: "*Your* judgments are remote to those who think they can get away with it."

This evil logic will be turned on its head when the sufferer asks God for help in the third section of the psalm. Evil ways will not prosper, despite what evildoers may think; God's judgments will come down to where we live.

His mouth is full of curses and deceit and op-
pression; under his tongue is trouble and wickedness.

This sentence catalogues the ways people intimidate, mislead, and overwhelm others. The wicked are "full" of what then overflows. Something "under the tongue" is ready to use at a moment's notice. The psalm gives categories, not specifics, inviting you to fill in the details.

Psalm 10 speaks from the standpoint of the innocent victim who relies on God. But sufferers must honestly ask themselves, "Am I more like my oppressor than I want to admit? Does God find bitterness and falsehood in me? Are there ways I act as if there is no God? Does my reaction to evil reveal my own evil, or a living faith?"[4] The apostle Paul cites this verse in Romans 3:10 to raise this humbling question. In a lengthy, direct challenge to every human being, Paul convicts every one of us of sin, and convinces us that our standing with God depends on what Jesus did. "Are we better than they? . . . There is none righteous, not even one. . . . For all have sinned and fall short of the glory of God, being justified as a gift by His grace through the redemption which is in Christ Jesus." The fair punishment for sin is capital punishment. Jesus, the only true innocent, took what I deserve (Rom. 3:25).[5]

Here is how Helen reflected on her experience. "I did not do the hateful things my husband did, but I spent years in bitterness and played the injured victim-doormat, with all the self-righteousness and self-pity of that role. I fantasized vengeance at times—even murder. Part of my silence came from living for my social reputation. I gave romantic fantasies air time in my mind. I often took refuge in junk food rather than in God. My husband intimidated and manipulated me; in those ways I was a victim. But at other times the easy way out shaped my choices. Yes, my husband sinned in dreadful ways, but Jesus' mercy has enabled me to face it with a growing measure of mercy. I have come to know God's love as refuge from my sufferings *and* my sins."

He sits in the lurking places of the villages. In the hiding places he kills the innocent. His eyes stealthily watch for the unfortunate. He lurks in a hiding place as a lion in his lair. He lurks to catch the afflicted. He catches the afflicted when he draws him into his net. He crouches, he bows down, and the unfortunate fall by his mighty ones.[6]

Evildoers "lurk." They conceal what they do, seeking to trap the innocent. Of course, with respect to God, none of us are innocents.

But on the human-to-human level, there *are* innocents. Helen was an innocent. A husband whose wife is abusive and irresponsible is an innocent. Children who are molested, beaten, or abandoned are innocents. Aging parents whose children neglect them are innocents. Victims of racism or auto theft or religious persecution are innocents. Jesus was an innocent. None of these deserves what he gets from the "man who is of the earth" (v. 18). You are meant to cry out, "Unfair! Outrageous!" and to feel the hair stand up on the back of your neck. Evil terrifies and intimidates the innocent and weak.[7]

He says to himself, "God has forgotten. He has hidden His face. He will never see it."

Evil people really think they'll never be called to account. Helen's husband was sure his mistresses and larceny could be kept out of sight. He believed a lie.

III. Cry to God: Act to Aid the Hurting (vv. 12–15)

Arise, O LORD. O God, lift up Your hand. Do not forget the afflicted.

The voice that said, "God, you seem distant," now cries, "God, be near." The voice that rehearsed trouble now begs that the trouble be dealt with. This God can "rise" and "lift his hand": he can remember—and do something. The wicked may think that God will never act. Believing sufferers may wonder (v. 1), but they call on him to do something. The previous ten verses communicated a dark world where the violator produces bleak fear in the victim. But now that world begins to crack open. Terrifying light begins to dawn on the self-absorbed mind of the wicked. Delightful light begins to dawn into the frightening world of the afflicted. The Lord misses nothing. He does not forget.

Why has the wicked spurned God? He has said to himself, "You will not require it." You have seen it, for You have beheld trouble and vexation to take it into Your hand.

God *has seen* the hurt and turmoil the wicked inflict. The dark threat thrives on concealment and the powerlessness of its victims, but it is completely visible to God. The thought processes and actions of evildoers are presented to God in urgent need and trust: "You see; you judge good and evil; you act." As Helen interprets her husband, she intercedes with God intelligently and forcefully.

The unfortunate commits himself to You. You have been the helper of the orphan.

God has been the helper of the helpless. He must become such again. This is no theoretical God. Human need seeks real divine help.

These sentences put the plight of the sufferer in very strong words. The "unfortunate" and "orphan" is the "hurting person," the helpless, needy, and forlorn. What do the needy need? Many forms of help may be timely. The church of Christ can help Helen in many practical ways. And because American society fosters a degree of social conscience, the legal system can help her find a measure of justice, protection, and recompense from her husband. Mercy ministries, social work, and advocacy for the powerless, poor, and disenfranchised are good things. But Psalm 10 drives home a bigger issue. First and finally, the needy need God. God runs his universe to ensure that in an evil world, no mere human advocacy can redress the full need.[8] Consider Jesus, the pioneer and perfecter of the life of faith: "into Your hands I commit My spirit" (Luke 23:46) and "for the joy set before Him [He] endured the cross, despising [thinking little of] the shame" (Heb. 12:2). Profound suffering needs one who will "wipe away every tear from their eyes; and there will no longer be any death; there will no longer be any mourning, or crying, or pain" (Rev. 21:4).

Break the arm of the wicked and the evildoer. Seek out his wickedness until You find none.

The helper of the weak is the destroyer of the abusive. The arm that once "caught" the afflicted will be snapped in two. The mind, tongue, and actions of "wickedness" will be annihilated. Here is a profound irony. The wrongdoer thinks that the Lord will not seek out his sins ("require" 10:13). But the sufferer calls on God to seek out sins until they can't be found because they have been obliterated.

Abusers think, "God won't require it," but when God acts, evildoers reap what they sow. The sufferer asks God to bring on the logical consequences: the arm that broke another will be broken. Throughout the Bible, the consequences of an evil act have a certain appropriateness. The punishment fits the crime. For example, when Israel turned to the idol gods of the surrounding nations, she came under the political power of those nations (Judg. 2–16).

But remember, this is a cry of faith, not pride. If I become the vindictive one, I assume that evils against me must be remedied by God right now. Faith trusts God's wrath in a different way. This is the cry of the weak one who trusts the Strong One, the hurting person who trusts the One who will make it all better. Helen can let go of her bitterness. She can refuse to play tit-for-tat with her husband in court. She can let go of the years of darkness, secrets, fear, and shame. She can trust someone else to make all wrongs right and get on with her life. The wrath of God is a central piece of the hope of God's people.[9]

IV. Confident Affirmation: The Lord Will Right Wrongs (vv. 16–18)

The LORD is King forever and ever. Nations have perished from His land.

This psalm ends with quiet confidence. God is a person with a name—Yahweh, I AM THAT I AM—who rules forever. He has proved it in history. Sufferers call on a God who has annihilated evildoers and idolaters. This King is now known as Jesus. He has redeemed the nations—Helen included—by perishing in the place of his elect. But those who reject him will cry, "Mountains, fall on us!" at their impending destruction.

Where do sufferers place their hopes? The first half of this statement is quoted in the New

Testament: "[The Lord] will reign forever and ever" (Rev. 11:15). Christ wins; evil loses. This is the indestructible foundation for human hopes, even when our schemes for earthly joy are shattered by sufferings.

> These inward trials I design,
> From sin and self to set thee free,
> To break thy schemes for earthly joy,
> That thou may'st find thy all in Me.
> John Newton

Here, too, the great divide among sufferers becomes obvious. The psalm writer, all God's people, Jesus, and Helen put their hopes in the right place, and come out in the right place. Other sufferers break when their schemes for earthly joy are broken. They come out vindictive, addicted, embittered, immoral, unbelieving, and greedy. The Lord will reign with his people; idolaters will perish.

O LORD, You have heard the desire of the afflicted.

Victims want many things: protection, relief, vindication, justice, and hope. The Lord hears such desires, for they reflect God's own intention. God is the righteous Judge who hears the cry of his chosen ones (Luke 18:1–8). But will the Lord find faith on the earth when he comes? Will afflicted ones rest their hopes on him? Are you in fact the "poor in spirit," one who knows your need and brings it to the Lord? Psalms never vindicate victims who act like the wicked themselves, plotting vengeance, thinking that "there is no God." The afflicted are believers who cry to the personal God on whom they rely.

We saw earlier that the wicked "boasts of his heart's desire." He is arrogant, autonomous, demanding. But "the desire of the afflicted" is heard because it is aligned with the purposes of the loving God. "This is the confidence which we have before Him, that, if we ask anything according to His will, He hears us. And if we know that He hears us in whatever we ask, we know that we have the requests which we have asked from Him" (1 John 5:14–15). Thomas Watson commented that "desires are the soul and life of prayer."[10] Equally, desires are the soul and life of wickedness. Understanding the difference is life for the soul!

You will strengthen their heart.

God acts first to strengthen sufferers inter-nally. If you "suffer in a Godward direction," he gives you hope. It is in the context of suffering that God strengthens hearts in many ways. The love of God pours out directly into the hearts of afflicted persons who rely on him in hope (Rom. 5:3–5). God becomes directly *known*— "seen"—in ways previously unimaginable (Job 42:5). Our foolishness is revealed, so that we might receive growing wisdom directly from God (James 1:2–5). We are remade into the image of Jesus and established in the love of God (Rom. 8:29, in the context of 8:18–39). We learn to trust and obey Jesus, who walked the path of unjust suffering *ahead* of us and now walks it *with* us (Heb. 4:14–5:9 and 12:1–11). Our self-centered cravings are revealed and our faith is purified and simplified (1 Peter 1:3–15). Helen trembles in the face of betrayal, but God can bring substantial joys out of her nightmare.

Here again, Jesus is the pioneer. His passion began with sorrow, betrayal, and abandonment:

- "Father, let this cup pass from Me."
- The silence of a lamb before its shearers.
- "My God, my God, why have You forsaken me?"
- "I am thirsty."

This sufferer loved his enemies, as we are called to do:

- "Today you will be with Me in paradise."
- "Father, forgive them, for they do not know what they are doing."
- "Woman, behold your son. . . . Behold your mother."

His passion ended in commitment and hope:

- "It is finished."
- "Into Your hands I commit My spirit."

Faith finds God in suffering, producing endurance, love, and hope. Psalm 10 is one part in the larger gospel whole, one piece of the experience of each God-centered sufferer.

You will incline Your ear to vindicate the orphan and the oppressed, so that man who is of the earth will no longer cause terror.

God not only strengthens hearts in suffering, he destroys the powers of evil. The weak will be vindicated. Yes, some people intimidate, but they will be destroyed, some sooner, some later, all sooner or later.

A marvelous promise closes this psalm: "That man who is of the earth may cause terror no more." People are fundamentally weak—mere clay, morning mist. An evildoer has a moment of power to hurt, but the God who is fundamentally strong will have the final say. That hope animates "groan[s] within ourselves" that everything will someday be renewed (Rom. 8:23). Alongside, the Holy Spirit "intercedes for us with groanings too deep for words" (Rom. 8:26). We will be delivered from all sin and misery. Every tear will be wiped away when evil is no more (Rev. 20–21).

Application: Make This Your Own

Read the psalm as a whole (see pages 1–3), turning it into your own words and thoughts.

I. Opening Cry: Where Are You? (v. 1)

1. Talk *to* God. Talk out loud. Many sufferers stay submerged in their thoughts and feelings, and stifle spoken prayer. Prayer means asking someone for help. Too often "prayer" is indistinguishable from thought life. "God" becomes blended with chaotic mental processes, rather than existing as a distinct person. But God is a person. Talk to him. Jesus prayed out loud with feeling: "He offered up both prayers and supplications with loud crying and tears to the One

able to save Him from death, and He was heard because of His piety" (Heb. 5:7). Cry out.

2. Psalm 22 captures in even greater detail the relationship between a sufferer and his God, who seems far away. It is even more explicitly Jesus' experience. After making Psalm 10 your own, do the same with Psalm 22. God will meet you in the integrity of your real life experience.

3. The Psalms are intended for use by groups of people, as well as by individuals. Who can pray with you? God does not intend you to fully resolve your struggles even in private with him. Join the people of God in a setting where your needs can be presented to God by others.

4. Matthew 26–27, Mark 14–15, Luke 22–23, and John 18–19 make it plain that Jesus not only experienced sufferings *like* yours, he experienced evil in *greater concentration*. In fact, he did it *for* you, and *on purpose*. And his *cry was answered*, as God delivered him in power: Matthew 28, Mark 16, Luke 24, John 20–21. Read a different version of the story each day. Think about these things.

II. Analyze Harmful People: They Are Proud, Willful, Godless, and Predatory (vv. 2–11)

1. Are you suffering? Have you been "burned" because someone else "burned" to do you wrong?

- Have you been verbally attacked, humiliated, treated with contempt, slandered?
- Have you been sexually manipulated, molested, seduced, raped?
- Have you been financially victimized?
- Have you been physically threatened, stalked, attacked, beaten, or tortured?
- Have you been a victim of prejudice regarding race, age, gender, ethnicity, economic status, disability, or religious faith?
- Have you faced a multitude of evils? Helen's circumstances fit the category "all of the above."

Describe what has happened to you: who, what, when, where, how, why. Talk it out with God in detail, according to the pattern of Psalm 10.

2. We are usually aware of what wrongdoers *do*, because that directly affects us. What does Psalm 10 say about how they *think*, what they *want*, what they *worship*, what they do *with God*? How does recognizing this Godward dimension help you when you face the sting of their actions? How does it make you less alone?

3. How have you sinned? Have you criticized, lusted, stolen, threatened, or been prejudiced? Do you lose sight of God and sink into unbelief? How do your sins come out in reaction to being sinned against? Remember, God has transformative purposes in the sufferings of those who love him.

4. What has Jesus Christ done to save sinners? Study 2 Corinthians 5:14–21 for the condensed version: Jesus has dealt with both sin's penalty and sin's perverse mastery. Study Romans 3:9–6:23 for the detailed version. You have been given an inexpressibly wonderful gift, and nothing can take it away. No suffering can separate you from God's love: Romans 8:18–39.

III. Cry to God: Act to Aid the Hurting (vv. 12–15)

1. What will Jesus Christ do to unrepentant sinners who harm God's children? Study 2 Thessalonians 1:6–10 for the condensed version. Study Revelation for the uncut version.

2. Talk *to* God. But don't babble. Talk intelligently, based on an understanding of God's reign of power and grace that deals with evil and suffering. Many sufferers simply writhe in pain and confusion. Jesus prayed knowing exactly

what he was saying, focused on obeying the will of the Father: "My Father, if it is possible, let this cup pass from Me; yet not as I will but as You will" (Matt. 26:39). He modeled the things he had taught his disciples to pray (Matt. 6:9–13). Don't grumble. Don't fall into the superstition of using fine-sounding religious phrases. Don't name and claim, thinking that your words pry goodies out of heaven. Don't think that piety can't ask for anything specific. Pray direct prayers pursuing God's will and glory.

3. Ask God to act: "Destroy evil and promote good." Prayer is not about working up some state of mind, though prayer does affect our state of mind, as Psalm 10 illustrates. Prayer goes to Someone you love and trust, asking for action and confessing faith.

IV. Confident Affirmation: The Lord Will Right Wrongs (vv. 16–18)

1. What truths do you need to affirm? Where can you find calm, strength, hope, and comfort? Begin where Psalm 10 begins. What else can you put in your confession of faith in the midst of trouble?

2. Ponder this (slightly modified) statement of faith from the sixteenth century Heidelberg Catechism:

What is your only comfort in life and in
death?

That I am not my own, but belong—
    body and soul,
    in life and in death—
to my faithful Savior, Jesus Christ.
    He has fully paid for all my sins with
        his precious blood,
    and has set me free from the tyranny of
        the devil.
    He also watches over me in such a way
    that not a hair can fall from my head
    without the will of my Father in
        heaven;
    in fact, all things must work together
        for my salvation.
Because I belong to him,
    Christ, by his Holy Spirit,
    assures me of eternal life
    and makes me wholeheartedly willing
        and ready
    from now on to live for him.

If you grasped these things with your whole heart, how would it affect the way you handle suffering?

3. David turned his suffering into words that have brought hope and guidance to countless

people for three thousand years. Can you turn your experience into a ministry of reaching out to others who suffer? God "comforts us in all our affliction so that we will be able to comfort those who are in any affliction" (2 Cor. 1:4).

Summary

Psalm 10 teaches us to think clearly and seek help from where help really comes. You need to THINK about what has happened. Who has mistreated you? What have they done? How do they think? What are they doing with God (not just with you)? Since evildoers are often deceitful (vv. 5 and 7), they can be hard to identify. Often the first people they deceive are their victims. See your danger for what it is.

You need to SEEK help. This help comes first and finally from the living God. He hears, helps, strengthens, and vindicates those who rely on him. If you look anywhere else first, you will set yourself up for a fall. You will get snared in bitterness and revenge (spurning God for *your* pride). You will flee in avoidance and addiction (spurning God for *your* false refuges and comforts). You will develop a perverted dependency on others (spurning God for *your* trust in man). Sadly, our culture has awakened countless people to think about what evildoers ("abusers") have done to them. But it has cast them upon their own resources as "abuse victims." Yet victims can properly understand their own sins and sufferings, and God's grace. They can learn the faith of Psalm 10 and find hope, mercy, and courage in dealing with evildoers.

As you seek the Lord, you will find that many secondary helps contribute to the healing process. There is a place to call the police, press criminal charges, pursue church discipline, seek counseling, weep with a friend, get financial advice, and so forth. The Lord is a refuge who leads us to rightly appropriate the many other helpers who can play a part in our lives—and to play a part for good in others' lives, as well. As Helen learns to think about evil and beseech God, she will also learn to participate in the community of God's people in a rich, immediate way. She'll have things to offer other sufferers down the road—a heart that has learned to think and pray Psalm 10, for example (a 2 Cor. 1:4 "comfort in any affliction"). What her husband meant for evil, God meant and works for good.

Notes

1 The translation that appears is largely from the New American Standard Bible (1995). I have made several minor alterations, breaking compound sentences into shorter sentences, and changing "mischief" to "trouble" in verses 7 and 14. The only substantial change is in the second half of verse 2, discussed in note 3.

2 This difficult sentence either means "the wicked *burn after* the afflicted" or "the wicked *burn* the afflicted." The first case describes the hostility and passion of harmful people. The second case describes the sufferer's hurt and fear. Either is consistent with the rest of Scripture. I will take it in the first sense, following this translation.

3 This is one place where I have departed from the NASB, which has "Let them [the wicked] be caught in the plots which they have devised." The Hebrew could be either further description of the wicked (as I have taken it) or a request to God that they reap what they sowed. Either is consistent with the rest of Scripture. A call for the wicked to reap what they sow occurs later in the psalm and will be discussed in section III.

4 In many psalms that lament suffering and cry for deliverance, the sufferer also confesses his own sins: 25, 38, 40, 69, 143.

5 Paul does not ignore the suffering of the innocent victim who loves God. He discusses this at length in Romans 8, quoting Psalm 44, another psalm of affliction, in 8:36. He embeds our sufferings in God's larger purposes.

6 "Mighty ones" might allude to the claws and fangs of the lion as it rips, kills, and feeds on its prey.

7 This psalm is not for those whose sense of "brokenness" primarily arises from their own thwarted lusts. It is for those who are truly "poor in spirit" and need God.

8 In Helen's case, the church did a wonderful job. But sufferers can still find hope and God's particular grace when normal social supports have been destroyed, as did Corrie ten Boom in *The Hiding Place*.

9 "Fire and brimstone" have fallen into disrepute in part because they are often only one-third understood. Yes, God delivers a *dreadful warning to the ungodly*. But destruction of evil is also the Lord's *loving rescue of his own people,* which generates hope amid affliction. (This is not inconsistent with loving and forgiving our enemies, and praying for their repentance; to do anything else would usurp God's right to judge [Rom. 12:14–21].) Judgment is also presented as God's *demonstration of his own glory and righteousness,* prompting wonder and rejoicing in those who love him. We will someday marvel at the God who brings full and final relief. (See the fire and brimstone of Gen. 19:24; Ps. 11:6; Ezek. 38:22; Rev. 14:10; 20:10; cf., 2 Thess. 1:3–10 and 2 Peter 2:6–10.)

10 Cited in Charles Spurgeon's *Treasury of David* regarding this verse.

David Powlison *is the editor of the* Journal of Biblical Counseling *and a member of the faculty and counseling staff at the Christian Counseling and Educational Foundation in Glenside, Pennsylvania.*

RCL Ministry Booklets

A.D.D.: Wandering Minds and Wired Bodies, by Edward T. Welch

Anger: Escaping the Maze, by David Powlison

Angry at God? Bring Him Your Doubts and Questions, by Robert D. Jones

Depression: The Way Up When You Are Down, by Edward T. Welch

Domestic Abuse: How to Help, by David Powlison, Paul David Tripp, and Edward T. Welch

Forgiveness: "I Just Can't Forgive Myself!" by Robert D. Jones

Guidance: Have I Missed God's Best? by James C. Petty

God's Love: Better than Unconditional, by David Powlison

Homosexuality: Speaking the Truth in Love, by Edward T. Welch

"Just One More": When Desires Don't Take No for an Answer, by Edward T. Welch

Marriage: Whose Dream? by Paul David Tripp

Motives: "Why Do I Do the Things I Do?" by Edward T. Welch

Pornography: Slaying the Dragon, by David Powlison